In The Land

Of The Rising Bun

A Selection of Comic Verse

By

Steven Walton

Foreword

Hi, best wishes to you all, and I hope you enjoy reading my book as much I`ve enjoyed writing it.

To let you know a bit about myself, one of my main interests is of anything old, from buildings to fossils, and everything in between, which I suppose includes me in there somewhere.

If I had to pick one of my favourite movies, it would be Mary Poppins. I find it such a creative work of art with a great story line for the whole family to enjoy. And I very much admire the people who put it all together back in 1964.

I very much enjoy delicious homemade cooking, courtesy of my lovely wife Judy, and not forgetting our loveable cat Smokey, who doesn`t cook by the way.

If you have bought my book, then thank you very much, but if you haven`t, I hope you still enjoy reading it.

Copyright © *Steven Walton,* 2024
All Rights Reserved

This book is subject to the condition that no part of this book is to be reproduced, transmitted in any form or means; electronic or mechanical, stored in a retrieval system, photocopied, recorded, scanned, or otherwise. Any of these actions require the proper written permission of the author.

Table of Contents

Introduction	1
Now I`m Really on A Roll	2
Faulty Showers	6
Put the Chilli in The Fridge	10
He`s The One for Bending Rules	14
I Don`t Like This Current Bunn!	19
The Antics Roadshow	23
Get To Grips With A Twix	27
I`ve Been Around The Milky Way	31
My Doctor Lives On Scribble Down	35
At Those Pit Stops I get Tired	38
Barking Mad	42
They`ve Hit the Bar Again	45
I Gave Some Chops To Missus Lamb	48
In the Land of The Rising Bun	51
Who Shot Rick O`Shea!	59
It`s Too Much for Me to Bare	65
For Broom the Bell Tolls	69
Shall I Do The Weather or Not	73
The Holly and Her Ivy	77
She Saw Through My Window Joke	80
I`ve Made A Pair Of Wig Slippers	84
I Need A Word in Your Beer	88
Is Spider Man A Stand Up Comic	92

Close Calls in The Queue	96
To the Loo Is A Trek	101
Who`s Driving Nora Batty	106
The Rock Feature	109
A Tale of Two Kitties	116
Let`s Enjoy A Happy Landing	120
I`ll Let My Rhubarb Do The Talking	125
Your Crackers My Lord	129
I Must Catch Up on Some Sauce	132
A Flush with The Law	136
Three Kind Mice, See How They Pun	140
Fifty Shades of Ray	145
The Out of Time Team	150
Saturday Plight Fever	154
Was It Wise To Go To Morecambe	158
Has My Talent Gone To Waste	162

Introduction

If you like
A laugh or two.
My comic verse
Will bring to you.
Chuckles long
Short and wide.
So, enjoy
The happy ride.

Now I`m Really on A Roll

*Doctor I`m
Now revealing.
Like a pencil
I am feeling.*
Right, I`ll work
On the basis.
You are like
All pencil cases.

Paper was
Your state of mind.
Last week
I did find.
So, my thinking
Would define.
You need
To draw a line.

*I was more
A betting slip.
The football kind
Doctor Tripp.
Which became
A real caper.
When it seemed
A headed paper.*

Have you any
Other issues.
Yes, I was
A box of tissues.
Then nose blowing
Had begun.
So, I went
On the run.

My ex-wife
I discovered.
Said I was
A pencil coloured.
Don`t take it
Though as red.
I can see
You`re easily led.

Are you sure
About your call.
I saw the writing
On the wall.
Our marriage though
I tried to mend.
With a rubber
On the end.

Arriving home
I was aloof.
And paper there
Was greaseproof.
With a pencil
There in place.
She'd disappeared
Without a trace.

And wallpaper
Doesn't agree.
Hang-ups keep
Affecting me.
Well, it seems
Very clear.
There's a pattern
Forming here.

That's why
A papering joke.
I never tell
To audience folk.
Maybe you
Could re-engage.
If you paced
Along the stage.

My latest date
Said one morning.
Cardboard cut-outs
Are so boring.
I`m sure
You`ll be ok.
No, she stood
Me up today….

Faulty Showers

Basil Fawlty
That is me.
We`ve come back
To Torquay.
The Devon coast
Is hard to beat.
And the bookies
Down the street.

Me and Cybil
Argue still.
She`s always been
A bitter pill.
Although she calls
People pet.
She`s the one
Who needs a vet.

Our new chef
By the way.
Never seems
Up with play.
I said we need
A Dover sole.
But he replied
What`s the role?

Manuel`s back
We stayed in touch.
And married now
His wife is Dutch.
But wearing clogs
Despite my pleas,
All we smell
Is edam cheese!

Polly`s now
By herself.
After problems
With her health.
And after going
Through the mill.
Too much wind
Is with her still.

The Germans got
The scenic table.
Taking towels
They were unable.
And after Hans
Did some posing.
Cybil liked
His lederhosen.

In the kitchen
There is trouble.
Our new chef
Has downed a double.
Needing coffee
Very strong.
Polly said
The kettle`s on.

The dining room
Is very busy.
As Polly starts
Feeling dizzy.
Are my mussels
Ready yet?
Your arms madam
Look all set.

Look all set!
What`s your name!
It`s Fawlty but
It works to blame.
Core dear
Can`t you wait!
We`ve a lot
On our plate!

*Is my duck
Cooking still.*
Would you like
Now the bill.
*What about
My scotch broth.*
I`m afraid
The scotch is off!

**I`m hungry!
So is Grace!**
But Manuel
Is off the pace!
**What`s he doing
On the floor!**
To Hans again
He mentioned the war.

Put the Chilli in The Fridge

*So, Ern
What`s the book?*
It`s written by
Professor Cook.
Famous Digs
From The Past.
*Some bedsits
Are quite a blast.*

*I was reading
Once a book.
When a spider
Came to look.
I couldn't seem
To concentrate.
Reading about
A soldier`s fate.*

*Him I pushed
As he rose.
Heading up
Towards my nose.*
Has it left
A mental scar.
*Yes, it was
A Bridge Too Far.*

Please Eric
Stop this lark!
Your stories never
Hit the mark!
Well, I passed
On Mastermind.
Every question
They could find.

How many bones
Has a chicken.
My brain
Is not for picking.
Guessing brings
Many woes.
I wonder if
The Parson knows.

Anger once
He displayed.
When raffle tickets
I mislaid.
Were you told
To get a grip.
No, he tore
Me off a strip.

The cheese salad
You behold.
Would`ve been
Better cold.
But room inside
The fridge had gone.
And someone left
The oven on.

But for heating
Food of course.
Microwaves
Deserve applause.
Unlike ours
I moaned about.
When yesterday
It clapped out.

Clapped out
That was clever.
You`re sounding
Daft as ever!
Are you sure
The turntable!
Hasn't got
A record label!

*Some Chinese men
Were very nice.
When fixing Uncle
Bens twice.
They're very helpful
When you ring.
Especially if
It's Mister Ping.*

*Would you like
A tea, Ern.*
There's a joke
For us to learn.
*Your join line
Showing through.
Milking that
I'd rather do.*

Who's waiting
At the door?
*It's Mister Ping
From number four.
With microwave
There to hand.
For a minute
He likes to stand.*

He`s The One for Bending Rules

Hello dear
Come in Brenda.
How you`re looking
Very slender.
Have you been
To a gym.
No, he`d gone
For a swim.

Last week
I made a joke.
To improve
His breast stroke.
Did he see
The funny side.
Yes, there was
Too much to hide.

Poor Jim
Lacking wealth.
Worries about
His sexual health.
When serving food
His partner Sue.
Gave him later
Her peas too.

*Then I told
Stanley clear.
There's too much
Length there dear.
Firm though
I would say.
Some of it
Gets in the way.*

*Comfy though
At the least.
But the nature
Of the beast.
Is for me
And snoring head.
It's too long
A sofa bed.*

*Although shorter
Was the old.
Stanley's rule
Should've told.
Measuring though
Wearing shades.
Must have used
Centigrades.*

Is it going
Back then love.
*I`m not sure
If that`s enough.
The only way
I stand to win.
Is to really
Trade him in.*

What`s he like
Around the house.
*Last week
He caught a mouse.
But it takes
A tour of duty.
Even when
He`s feeling fruity.*

Often George
Is very slow.
Plenty ebb
But not the flow.
*If bath time
You`ve never tried.
You might catch
A rising tide.*

When we get
To waters deep.
Usually then
He falls asleep.
I once used
Sensual oil.
Until he rubbed it
On his boil.

Meals on Wheels
He`s started doing.
And he seems
Over the moon.
As he gets
Such a thrill.
Saving on
Our shopping bill.

Feeling hungry
Was his cry.
So, he tried
A shepherd`s pie.
Complaints though
Did begin.
When he gave
A sheepish grin.

He was moving
Very slow.
Loading up
His car you know.
Then like
It was a race.
He was told
To leave the plaice.

Did he soon
Drive away.
Yes, he left
There OK.
But without
The cod in sauce.
Which he`d eaten
Early doors.

But everything
Seems OK.
He was told
Yesterday.
By the boss
Don`t forget.
Your just desserts
Soon you`ll get….

I Don`t Like This Current Bunn!

Teaching people
How to drive.
Must include
Staying Alive.
Meeting though
Brenda Bunn!
Madness went
To number one!

Starting her
Lesson four.
I was feeling
Still unsure.
When heading for
A T-junction!
Cold toast
She was munching!

Finding this
Pizza freak's
Very cheesy
When she speaks.
Popping then
Another pill!
Went clutching
Down a hill!

Yesterday
I nearly weed.
Now she's getting
Up to speed.
As crossroads
In my sights!
Pictured me
The last rights!

Her brother sits
By her side.
And the other
Day I cried!
Don`t forget
That level crossing!
When she gave
Her lips a glossing!

Moving away
Rather quick!
She was pushing
On the stick!
Telling me
On certain nights!
How she works
The red lights!

Her concentration
Was n't good!
Especially where
People stood!
After though
Looking blank!
Picked up at
The taxi rank!

Looking at
The clutch pedal.
Saying I
Deserve a medal.
Brenda said
I agree.
Awarding me
A KFC!

Baking cakes
Left a dent!
When I wondered
What she meant!
Saying her
Inner soul!
Wants to make
A Mini roll!

Driving further
Down the street.
After chewing
On a sweet.
She made
Another stop.
Then offered me
A pear drop.

After starting
Off again.
She drove along
A bus lane!
Rubber coming
There to burn!
Nearly bought
A fare return!

Lesson four
Was complete.
Then chewing on
Another sweet.
Told me
This weekend.
She'll enjoy
A Fisherman`s Friend.

The Antics Roadshow

This roadshow's
In the mix.
Watching out
For certain tricks.
Like heading for
Camera two.
After they've
Jumped the queue.

Although paintings
Are a must.
I'm careful
Who I trust.
This Constable
Country scene.
Was framed by
A Mister Bean.

This painting's
Very striking.
Would there be
A family likening.
Oh, I see
Yes of course.
But what if someone`s
On the horse.

Here is some
Of Nelson's hair.
Nothing really
Could compare.
Though saving us
From defeat.
Split ends
He couldn't beat.

Station clocks
Rare in style.
Can be worth
Quite a pile.
But I've really
Sealed its fate.
It's British Rail
And running late.

Thunderbirds
Were good fun.
And they`ll all here,
Except for one.
But seeing Virgil,
Doubt remains.
Are they only
Missing Brains.

Listening to
A certain Mabel.
Lacking manners
At the table.
Tried hard
To reason why.
It wasn't bought
From MFI.

Viewing through
This eye piece.
On a pier
Would release.
Butlers watching
Full of glee.
Through where
The key should be.

These glasses were
Napoleon's pair.
So, they are
Extremely rare.
And after reading
Maps all wrong.
I know where
He should've gone.

Filming now
Had better stop.
For a coffee
I shall pop.
I'm receiving
Quite a glare.
Mabel`s bringing
Now a chair….

Get To Grips With A Twix

This evening
I bring to you.
A more chocolate
Point of view.
Then you`ll find
Your neighbours sweet.
And make it more
A Quality Street.

Chocolate judging
Left a scar.
When someone took
Away my bar.
Leaving then
After Eight.
One less Topic
To debate.

Although a person
Took a risk.
Eating my,
Bourbon bisc.
What`s the point
Of being suggestive.
As by now
Will be digestive.

A Chocolate Orange
Causing toil.
Could be just
The perfect foil.
When she`s cooked
A decent meal.
She might start
To have appeal.

Is your preference
Milk or plain?
Has your Time Out
Gone again?
Do Double Deckers
Get you going?
Are your Snickers
Nearly showing?

So, you see
This chocolate night.
I could be
Your guiding light.
But to make
The power run.
The button is
A chocolate one.

If you`re feeling
All at sea.
Having a Picnic
You could be.
Then Ripple on
The river Thames.
In Smartie pants
From M&M`s.

Although my wife
Is quite a dear.
But doesn`t Whispa
In my ear.
If in Turkish
You Delight.
I am free
On Tuesday night.

If It Was
The Milky Way,
Would her brother
Be OK.
I`m scared
Of taking knocks.
So there`d be
No Dairy Box.

If Chocolate Fingers
Often break.
When you`re only
Half awake.
And your Kat
Is just a Kit.
Be careful not
To lose a bit.

When the garden
You are in.
Snail finding
May begin.
Walking then
As you do.
A Crunchie moment
May ensue.

Needing soon
A tasty beer.
The Star Bar
I`m seeing clear.
If though
The night is long.
A different Planet
I`ll be on.

I`ve Been Around The Milky Way

Delivering milk
Is what I do.
To the likes
Of me and you.
I suppose we are
A dying breed.
Yet those housewives
Have the need.

Bacon, eggs
We sell the lot.
All that walking
Makes me hot.
Not to mention
One of course.
Who does me breakfast
With some sauce.

Twice a week
She oils her pan.
Knowing I`ll be
A hungry man.
And as the eggs
Are paid by me.
Her range is always
Nice and free.

When a lady
Jumps her horse.
Her rear
Changes course.
With me whipping
She did mock.
But I`d rather
Beat the clock.

Over poles
Does she fly.
With her tee shirt
Pulling high.
But despite
Those extra pounds.
Showed me once
Her two clear rounds.

Another lady
Leaves a note.
And she`d always
Get my vote.
Very often
I do dream.
About her use
Of all that cream.

After writing
Legislate.
As she`s now
A Magistrate.
Now that policeman
Lives next door.
She`s more familiar,
With the law.

When calling there
At number one.
Role- playing
Had begun.
After Licence
Victuallers.
He took down
Her particulars.

To a farm
I have to go.
The farmers wife
I used to know.
After working
Once her land.
Offered me
Today a hand.

We were in
The milking shed.
With the plough men
Joe and Fred.
And now I`ve seen
Her weekly yield.
She`s the leader
In the field.

That Magistrate
Left a note.
So, I neatly
Parked my float.
As her writing
It did state.
Her cream was nearly
Out of date….

My Doctor Lives On Scribble Down

I`m a doctor
On the go!
Meeting every
So and so!
Not to mention
Taking blood!
And yesterday
We had a flood!

Telling me
They`re going mad.
Seems to be
The latest fad.
Calmly though
I do remind.
That It`s all
Just in the mind.

Sick note
Is here again.
But this time
I shall explain.
With attendance
Getting worse.
I`ll have to find
A different nurse.

Hoarders need
Delicate care.
When stacking things
Everywhere.
And yesterday
Missus Miles.
Needed something
For her piles.

A man feeling
Very low.
Wearing creases
Would you know.
Couldn`t seem
To take on board.
His iron needs
To be restored.

People say
I`m Covid smug.
But I really
Love to hug.
I only get
A warm embrace!
When the wife
Is off her face!

A lady said
Paper clips.
Tasted very
Nice with chips.
So, I said
Missus Fryatt.
Don`t forget
Your staple diet.

Yesterday
A cleric scholar.
Asked for
A surgical collar.
Then after another
Painful sound.
Said the Lord
Will turn it around.

Gloves here
Arriving light.
Are for left
But not the right.
So later on
I shall pop
To a second
Hand shop....

At Those Pit Stops I get Tired

Welcome back
To Formula Two.
Where the start
Is nearly due.
Banking Basil`s
Here with me.
Spilling most
Of his tea.

As for racing
You do live.
A real buzz
It all must give.
Well yesterday
I took a spin.
My helmet had
A bee get in.

After starting
Down the straight.
What`s been
The worst of late.
Knowing by
The first bend.
A penny I
Forgot to spend.

Has there been
A moment though.
When you really
Stole the show.
The safety car
I used to drive.
I crashed it back
At corner five.

Racing though
From a boy.
What`s the part
You least enjoy.
Pit stops
Are a strain.
Waving to
My partner Jayne.

Is your lady
Here today.
No, she`s dancing
Far away.
But she makes
A proposition.
When she's in
The pole position.

Have you any
Lucky charms.
*Coal hanging
From my arms.*
Please now
Do explain.
*For driving in
The pit lane.*

This circuit's
Kind of new.
Have you fully
Ran it through.
*Although I need
To make amends.
In the bath
I got the bends.*

Would you say
Basil mate.
Your IQ
Isn`t great.
*No, I`d say
That is wrong.
Unless the queue
Is very long.*

And lastly for
Your fans today.
What's the message
You would say.
If a bath
You take tonight.
An extra lap
Might well excite....

Barking Mad

This ogre dog,
Takes me far.
So, I drive him
In the car.
With his jaws
Kind of knocking.
Seems to like
The central locking.

Thinking I`m
His sugar daddy.
He`s become
My golf caddy.
Then when resting
In between.
Did a long one
On the green.

His every meal
Is like a feast.
Weighing a ton
This giant beast.
Knowing he`ll
Never starve.
And when I tripped
He seemed to laugh.

Rolf is not
An easy dog.
Making life
A real slog.
Even when
I find his stick.
Always has
A bone to pick.

He pulls along
My hands weak.
Hiding somewhere
Should I seek?
Wishing so
To be alone.
From this brute
That`s overgrown.

Certain trees
Come in view.
When he has
Some jobs to do.
One was never
Quite the same.
A Weeping Willow
It became.

Yesterday
When playing tricks.
I imagined
Chasing sticks.
And after meeting
Up with Joyce.
I seemed to have
A Husky voice.

Now though,
It`s time for home.
Where I`ll write
Another poem.
Then after finding
Where he`s sat.
I`ll write about
Our pesky cat.

They`ve Hit the Bar Again

This football team`s
A boozy lot.
So, I`ve come
To stop the rot.
Although drinking
Is their theme!
They really are n't
The Bristol Cream!

Our striker
Lost a yard.
Finding games
Very hard.
But after drinking
Special Brew.
Started scoring
Quite a few.

Number eight
On the whole.
Never fancied
Any role.
Then became
A crowd pleaser.
Thanks to
Bacardi Breezer.

Our skipper takes
A different stance.
Doing his silly
Robot dance.
Looking though
More bionic.
Vodka is
His only Tonic.

Our winger`s
Very slow.
Lacking pace
And full of woe.
But after drinking
With his chums.
A rum chaser
He becomes.

Although our keeper
I`ve a hunch.
Never fancies
Any Punch.
Bishop`s Finger
Now he drinks.
Might just earn
A point he thinks.

Number ten,
I`m very sure.
Couldn`t hit
A barn door.
And even though,
He runs a lot.
Whisky is
His favourite shot.

Number seven
Got depressed.
When a scout
Was unimpressed.
But after drinking
Speckled Hen.
He was quickly
Spotted then.

Winning games
And bearing fruit.
Is making us
More resolute.
And I really
Found the knack.
When I had
A Scrumpy Jack....

I Gave Some Chops To Missus Lamb

We`re patrolling
Just about.
As Jones thought
He'd seen a kraut.
But what seemed
A German salute.
Was a scarecrow
In a suit.

Private Pike
On edge he spoke.
Said he's read
Of scarecrow folk.
Thinking it was
A clever decoy.
But he's such
A stupid boy!

Listen men!
We're running late!
That artillery gun
We must locate!
But Captain surely
What`s the hurry?
Your shiny head`s
Because you worry.

Walker you'll
Pay for that!
I'm tired of
Your cheeky chat!
Leave him Jones
This I'll deal!
But he needs,
Cold, hard steel!

Walker's causing
This commotion.
Captain there's
Some men approaching.
And they're wearing
German grey.
Put it up them!
All the way!

No Jones
Don't be rash.
It's that Heinkel
We saw crash.
Don't panic! some Germans
Are coming this way!
Don't panic! they're coming!
Don't panic! I say!

How many
Are there Pike?
*Two or three
It's looking like.
I don't think
They will attack.
But Jones mustn't
Cut them slack.*

**Speaking Captain
If I may.**
Yes Jones
They've gone away.
Then we'll search
Until we bust!
But no bayonet
Upper thrust!

*Panic not
Me this time.
I`m feeling
In my prime.
They can't escape
Their fate is sealed.
Look for scarecrows,
In the field….*

In the Land of The Rising Bun

Evening there
It`s morning still.
Unless I haven't
Took my pill.
Are they good
For sleeping tight.
No, the sheep
Go out at night.

After digging
Up some roots.
I was given
Them in Boots.
Do they have
A bitter taste.
No, they`re better
Whisky laced.

Changing clocks
Is nearly here.
But mine arrived
New this year.
The village idiot
Is that you?
People tell me
That is true.

In which one
Do you reside?
I really
Can't decide.
Have you got
A garden gate.
Only when
I'm walking straight.

Living close
To Maxwell House.
We get visits
From a mouse.
Where's it near
Fordham Gap.
Where coffee stains
Are on our map.

Tell me then
What's your name?
Tyler's what
Some people claim.
Watt was mine
From a boy.
I don't know
Was it Roy?

No, my name
Is Watt you see.
*I`ve been looking
At a tree.*
No, my name
Is really Watt!
*Was it Beech
Now I've forgot.*

Are you seeking
Idiot roles.
*MP's lose them
Through some moles.*
So, on doors
Would you clout?
*Only if
They were out.*

*The village clerk
Saw my claim.
And the letters
After my name.*
Which I bet
You did invent.
*No, I get
Behind with rent.*

The Round Table
I applied.
Before the leader
Went and died.
*Was he then
A certain friend.*
Yes, he sat
At the end.

*Is that why
Your meeting clicked.*
And that short
Straw, I picked.
Winning's easy
Come to that.
When it's hidden
In my hat.

*My house move
From number one.
Should've been
Sooner done.
A holiday home
Around the bay.
But they never
Went away.*

I'm worried about
My urgent letter.
I've applied
To buy a sweater.
I sent it by
The second post.
But the box
Is on the coast.

*When judging wine
At the fete.
I was choosing
Three from eight.*
Did the winner
Start to boast.
*It was me
I drank the most.*

*My wife's gone
To pastures new.
So, I'm left
Without a clue.*
Did you have one
To begin.
*Yes, I liked
Her sheepish grin.*

*A caravan
Is where I live.
And I'm trying
To forgive.
Squatting's really
All I know.*
Why is that
The ceiling's low.

Was her leaving
On the cards.
*She'd been cheating
By some yards.
Then she claimed
A full house.
But we only
Had the mouse.*

*Once she made
A Shepherd's pie.
But she never
Told me why.
Then she said
When drinking punch.
She enjoyed
A Plough Mans Lunch.*

Getting Toed
In the hole.
Wasn't good
For my soul.
When my usual
Drinking night.
Caused the wife
Again, to spite.

Did you then
Make a stand.
Sitting down
Is never grand.
And walking isn't
Good to do.
Especially when
She's followed through.

You could eat
Tonight, with us.
With her cooking
Being a plus.
That sounds,
Really good.
If steaks don't
Taste of wood.

We better drink
Scrumpy first.
As I have
A mighty thirst.
And she's cooking
Something slick.
Beef stew with
An extra kick.

Who Shot Rick O`Shea!

So, Ern
Here we go.
Starting now
Another show.
Shall I take it
From the top.
For a laugh
Let it drop.

Why is it
Every time!
On this stage
We talk in rhyme!
Wig wearing
Seems a curse.
Maybe you`ve
Become averse.

Can`t you find
A different groove!
Then your acting
Might improve!
I once played
Farmer Bart!
The cow herding
Stand in part!

Then years ago
To fill a gap!
What about
That school of tap!
Well, I never
Really shone.
I couldn't seem
To turn it on.

At least here
At ITV.
The canteen food
Is always free.
Though like
The BBC I`d say.
You get repeats
During the day.

Who`s appearing
Here tonight.
Des O`Connor`s
Booked a flight.
Singing his
Latest song.
Where Did
It All Go Wrong.

Eric we
Can`t delay!
It`s time for
My western play.
Whisky will
Be drunk a lot.
Followed by
A rifle shot.

Buck Marshall`s
Who I`ll be.
Hoping Apache`s
Soon will flee.
Well after seeing
Your war dance.
You`ll need
A different stance.

Will The Shadows
Be here soon.
Playing their,
Apache tune.
Hank Marvin`s
Feeling stiff.
After falling
Over a Cliff.

Clint Eastwood
Who I`m fond.
Has arrived
Across the pond.
If gun slinging
Happens Buck.
I`ll be ready
With a duck.

Des dancing
In the heat.
Maybe sounds
Incomplete.
He`ll become
A singing Jan.
Then he`ll need
To bring his fan.

You`re playing
Rick O`Shea.
A pistol shooter
By the day.
What about,
The evening time.
You and Jan
Will make it rhyme.

I enjoyed
The dress rehearsal.
*What about
Your role reversal!
Every time
You wear a frock!
The film crew
Go into shock!*

Please Eric
Give it a rest.
*You'll never
Pass the test!
And stage hand
Poor old Burt!
Spilled coffee
Down his skirt!*

Today you're
A cattle thief.
Who will later
Come to grief.
So, Dodge City
Here we are.
With cameras rolling
Near and far.

I`m feeling
Quite astute.
Are you ready
For the shoot.
No but
Before you run.
Quickly Annie
Get your gun….

It`s Too Much for Me to Bare

Your appointment
Missus Hart.
Has arrived
For the part.
She seems though
Quite a prude.
For a play
That`s in the nude.

I`m hoping
She`ll abide.
No one else
Has applied.
Except a man
Who did insist.
I put him on,
A short list.

Missus Hart
Pleased to meet.
Would you like
A medium sweet.
Cheers then
Mister May.
Or bottoms up
Should we say?

Right then
Let`s have a look.
You once sung
In Jungle Book.
Yes really
With some ease.
Was it Bare
Necessities.

Furniture
Is what I sell.
Acting though
I love as well.
I`m afraid
There`ll be no drawers.
Nor a French
Dresser of course.

After turning
Twenty- four.
I played
An Indian squaw.
The non speaking
One I feel.
Running Bear
Would be ideal.

I`m grateful
To be here.
But I need
To be sincere.
I`m looking for
A bigger part.
*Well, you`ll meet
Our charming Bart.*

*All the cast
I depend.
Have a means
To an end.
Including now
Comic Roy.
Stand up
He does enjoy.*

*Although I won
An accolade.
Producing Privates
On Parade.
After maybe
Treading boards.
Have you ever
Won awards.*

Even though
I won some praise.
When appearing in
The Summer Haze.
The last part
With Mister Dean.
Meant I was
Barely seen.

For Broom the Bell Tolls

Buttons is
The part I play.
In Cinderella
Every day.
But with flies
I like to skip.
So, I`d rather
Be a zip.

Baron Hard Up
Was my boss.
But my leaving
Was his loss.
When Town Crying
By and large.
He never paid
My call out charge.

When Cinderella
Was my catch.
We did strike
A perfect match.
But my presence
Often hinders.
So that`s why
They call her Cinders.

Her cruel
Ugly sisters.
Do resemble
Nasty blisters.
Drinking scenes
They have mastered.
And they`re often
Very plastered.

They mistreat
Hard Up`s daughter.
Like a lamb
To the slaughter.
She would like
To meet the prince.
Although he walks
With a mince.

Cinders washed
Many dishes.
Then received
A choice of wishes.
In this water
You`ll discover.
I`m your Liquid
Fairy Mother.

*At that greatest
Ball I`ve found.
Your good luck
Will come around.
But if you pass
The midnight peel.
You will turn
Into a wheel.*

The ugly sisters
Hear of this.
And the cleaning
She will miss.
So, with dust
On every ledge.
They decide
To make a pledge.

They will hide
Her shoes away.
Then at home
She`ll have to stay.
But old walkers
From the past.
Delivered cheese
And bunion fast.

So, the ball
Cinder`s at.
Where a mother
Told her that.
When I take
The goat to sea.
The kids nanny
You could be.

The Charming Prince
Then she met.
Told her that
He was a vet.
Then lifting her
Like a clown.
Joked about
Putting her down.

That Fairy Mother
In a verse.
Was no better
Than of worse.
As midnight passed
With a fluster.
The Prince turned
Into a duster.

Shall I Do
The Weather or Not

Morning all
Young and old.
Here`s the weather
So, I`m told.
Hoping It`s
A piece of cake.
And the drizzle
Isn`t fake.

Depending on
Your hymn sheet.
Should we joke
About the heat.
As church goers
Funny smiles.
Gather in
The Scilly Isles.

Rain though
Will spread tonight.
From Cardigan Bay
To The Isle of Wight.
From The Needles
It will grow.
But Jersey wasn`t
Mentioned though.

If romancing
In a tent.
Rain is moving
Up to Gwent.
And if tonight
Things are grey.
She might prefer
The Pennine Way.

The morning after
Coming through.
You might find
A spot or two.
Shining like
Red October.
Especially on
Cliff`s at Dover.

If in Gretna
You were green.
A doctor then
You would`ve seen.
Trying hard
There to spot.
On his chart
The whether or not.

On northern hills
There`ll be rain.
Unless you`re heading
Off to Spain.
I though
Follow my nose.
So that`s where
A me goes.

In Holmfirth
It would appear.
Foggy days
Were crystal clear.
Though Nora said
When Compo kissed.
Maybe one day
He`ll be missed.

If you`ve had
A whisky blend.
Thinking snow
Is in Southend.
Then you try
A different kind.
Scotch mist
At least you`ll find.

On the steamy
Southern coast.
Where saucy cards
I like to post.
When the rain
Passed OK.
Her mother said
She`s on her way.

After hearing
Icy path.
Someone here
Is having a laugh.
So, I`ll read
Between the lines.
Now I`ve had
A couple of wines.

The Holly and Her Ivy

Christmas day
Is full of riddles.
As I'm eating
Cheesy nibbles.
The open fire's
Very hot.
And roasted nuts
I've also got.

Although my wife
Is quite a dish.
Her mother's drinking
Like a fish.
Including now
My home brew.
Is going down
Her Jaws Two.

The rose's
Nicely chilled.
With her glass
Over filled.
And now Titanic`s
Gone to bed.
The kitchen sink
She'll watch instead.

Looking then
So remote.
Channel hopping
Got my goat.
Then after drinking
Nothing strong.
Went back
To Carry On.

Her present
Was a flop.
A jumper from
The charity shop.
Which I know
I`ll never wear.
It was mine
I took it there.

Cracker pulling
Ivy Mellor.
Then became
A tree feller.
With a bauble
In her grey.
As the King
Had his say.

Waking later
To rescind!
Soon became
An ill wind!
Sitting there
Lacking grace!
As I sprayed
Around the place!

Knocking back
The Irish Cream.
She was drinking
To extreme.
Her river dance
Wasn't good!
In a puddle
There she stood!

Enjoying now
A tasty brew.
I think about
Her husband who.
Never drinks
Any liquor.
Though enjoys
Being a vicar.

She Saw Through My Window Joke

Cleaning windows
For a living.
Can be really
Unforgiving.
Unless we`re talking
Naughty Sue.
Then I usually
See it through.

Loving cats
The pair do.
It`s where
Their life is true.
And selling cat food
Really pays.
So left their jobs
In litter trays.

At the bank
Where I clean.
When the boss
Missus Green.
Mentioned once
The overdraft.
Close the window
Then I laughed.

A stern look
I was given.
But was not
Propeller driven.
Viewing though
Her upper deck.
Took some pain
From my neck.

Then she spoke
About arrears.
So, I explained
How wax appears.
Although she laughed
When I said it.
Still wouldn`t
Give me credit.

Pizza Parlour`s
Missus Hines.
Likes to write
Some comedy lines.
When I joked
About her bun.
Said she couldn`t
Top that one.

Still here
At number four.
A ginger Tom
Is at the door.
Her cat food`s
A world beater.
Or he`s come
To read her meter.

She could never
Understand.
Her peacock dress
Wasn`t grand.
So, her husband
Said OK.
Parrot fashion
Is the way.

Their parrot`s
In the wrong.
After stringing
Me along.
Really wishing
He`d get knotted.
Then become
A lesser spotted.

Although he chirps
Pale Face.
Approaching is
A different case.
The parrot`s told
Husband Lee.
Up the ladder
What I see….

I`ve Made A Pair
Of Wig Slippers

So, I see
You`ve got it then.
Yes, I wear
A wig now Ben.
But I`m really
Not at ease.
So can we change
The subject please.

Yes of course,
Straight away.
My daughter`s bought
A car today.
Has she found
A house yet.
Yes It`s in
New Barnet.

Sorry John
I didn't mean.
Let`s keep it
All Serene.
My wife
Is choosing frocks.
For a part
In Goldilocks.

Your company
Did it sell?
*Yes, it went
Very well.
A wealthy person
Saved the day.
He's a big wig
So, they say.*

*Once again
I didn't mean.*
What about
Your brother Ian!
Is he still,
In Lancashire!
Being a butler
To that peer!

*Yes that's
Still the case.
At that mansion
Wigan Place.
Wigan Place
Mm that's the one.
Would you like
A home-made bun?*

To uni then
He didn't go!
*No, he's always
Short of dough.
Thinking on
Ahead of that.
Best to keep it
Under your hat.*

*Mm let's hear
The latest news.
My new radio
I shall use.
An MP's
Fate is sealed.
A cover up
Has been revealed.*

That's it!
I've had enough!
*Please forgive me
For this stuff.
Some tasty beer
We could enjoy.
Down the local
Sailor Boy.*

*A country singer's
There tonight.
And I've heard
She sounds alright.
And I promise
Not to say.
Things about
Your wig OK.*

Yes ok
With a beer.
Some country hits
I'd like to hear.
*If she does
Dolly Parton`s too.
She might do one
Just for you....*

I Need A Word in Your Beer

Pud evening all
In my adverse.
I've a problem
Getting worse.
Horsing greatly
Me castration.
Suffering from
Pismunciation.

Although I come
From finer stock.
I don't really
Have the knock.
Stuck inside
This living hall.
Making little
Fence at all.

Supermarkets
Are a threat.
As in puddles
I do wet.
When basking for
Sliced bread.
I kept doing
Pees instead.

Neck out girls
So contrite!
Often take
The miss outright!
When I said
Parrots and caulie!
One replied
Pretty Polly!

After being
Friendly faced!
She was clearly
Toothpaste!
Though my wife's
Supporting quest.
Even belps,
When she's pressed.

Asking for
Red Leicester bees.
Must've sounded
More shy knees.
And I hadn't
Staple lated.
I prefer it
When it's mated.

At least I've
A rusted friend.
Who oak vat's
A Scottish blend.
And expanding
Mr. Willoughby.
Showed me around
His nudist Hilary.

Cycle hiding
Is a no.
But one day
I had to go.
Changing gears
Was a middle.
When I slipped,
Off the piddle.

At the yokel
Swimming pool.
I was trying
To lay it cool.
Until the wife
The other week.
Nearly put me
Off my streak.

Swimming lessons
Are a must.
And every time
She tries her bust.
The splashing water
Made us grin.
Though my south
Took some in.

After finding
Better digs.
To the shop
We're smoking figs.
Hurry powder's
On her list.
And pop alongs
She can't resist.

Is Spider Man A Stand Up Comic

Spiders never
Frighten me.
Some though
Can`t bare to see.
To my house
They come at Will.
But they never
Go to Jill.

Often coming
Here to flock.
They`re attracted
To a clock.
The poorly one
Seemed to know.
The cuckoo said
It`s time to go.

Grandfather
Rung a chime.
As I told
A nursery rhyme.
Then a spider
Feeling pain.
Saw the mouse
Come down again.

A spider walking
In the hall.
Turned himself
Into a ball.
By our cat
He was found.
So no longer
Is around.

After coming
Through a hole.
One seemed
A troubled soul.
Then I wept
A single tear.
As he jumped
Into my beer.

Bath time
To disengage.
Soon became
A spider stage.
One dancing
Very bold.
Must`ve thought
The tap was cold.

Wet gloss
Looking neat.
Had a spider
Spread his feet.
Blowing him
Though I`d say.
Didn`t really
Save the day.

I`m afraid
He couldn`t win.
After landing
In the tin.
Brilliant white
Was he most.
Looking like
A spider ghost.

Cards dealt
Around the fire.
Led me to
A funeral pyre.
One glowing
Near the pot.
Found the poker
Very hot.

So, from
Here in Crawley.
Is the ending
To my story.
If you visit
Have no fear.
Spiders die
When they come here.

Close Calls in The Queue

Hello dear
Thought I`d call.
Don`t cook
For me at all.
I`m today
Not a winner.
Feeling like
A dog`s dinner.

The man behind
On his phone.
Was trying hard
To pick a bone.
In this queue
Standing tall.
Is making now
Another call.

Hi James
It's Simon here.
I`m waiting for
The bus dear.
How was your
Latest date.
A long queue
Is never great.

Where did
You actually meet.
*The supermarket
Down the street.*
Were you dressed
For a ball.
*No, they're best
Overall.*

You're excited
I can hear.
*Yes, I found
The melons dear.*
So, she didn't
Make you wait.
*One though
Was second rate.*

Wasn't that
Quite inept.
*No that's where
The pears are kept.*
Did you really
Have some fun.
*Yes, I got
The photos done.*

Well, that sounds
A decent bet.
*And I got
Potatoes pet.*
Then she started
Acting hyper!
What's her name?
Maris Piper.

Then later she
Reminded you!
King Edward she`s
Related to!
What about
Some decent pins.
*They`re delicious
In their skins.*

*Yes, I found
My favourite soup.*
What! she doesn't
Use a scoop!
Dogs really
I detest!
*Cock-a-leekie
Is the best.*

So, the waiter
With no hair.
What's that love
Biscuits where?
Served rice
Looking mouldy
Called him what!
Garibaldi.

Later she
Was kicking butts!
And we needed
Ginger nuts.
So, what damage
Has been done!
They've replaced
The two for one.

She's a little
Cow I feel.
No, I couldn`t
Get the veal.
Then she spoke
Indiscreet.
And wanted what?
Sausage meat.

The fresh plaice
Wasn't great.
But you still
Took the bait.
Yes, some crabs
And a kipper.
Oh, she's got
A little nipper.

Yes, I got
Sliced bread.
Well, I hope
It doesn't spread.
It's a peril
Of a thought.
Bloomers though
Came up short.

Single cream
By the way.
Was removed
Yesterday.
I'd forget it
My old mate.
She was best
Before the date.

To the Loo Is A Trek

Painting Views
Is the show.
Where we help
The amateur grow.
Our weekly guest
We random pick.
Who's oil painting
Could be slick.

What a name
This one's got.
Does he really
Paint or not.
There are doubts
About his spec.
Here is To
The Loo`s A Trek.

Your name
Is very odd.
Yes, it was
My father Rod.
He left me
Feeling small.
So, a shrink
I had to call.

After moving
Up to Clyde.
Our toilet was
Too far outside.
And dad said
Blooming heck!
To the loo
Is a trek!

So, this name
I can't defend!
Nearly sent me
Round the bend!
As my father
With a laugh!
Led me up
The garden path!

I've just felt
A lightning strike.
Toulous-Lautrec
Your name is like.
In that bar
I would agree.
Getting legless
There you see.

Have you then
A certain style.
Well, I have
A friendly smile.
French impressions
Do you seek?
No, my accent
Is too weak.

Is there something
Maybe quaint.
That you'd really
Love to paint.
The Eiffel tower's
Silhouette form.
At sunrise
Before it's warm.

You`re sounding
Very sure.
So, what are
You waiting for.
I do love
The French delights.
Yes, but I'm
Scared of heights.

Oh, I see
Like I thought.
You're a painter
Of a sort.
Yes, my work
Is nothing great.
I just paint
And decorate.

You`ve been
Skirting around.
Yes but
I`m fairly sound.
My roller painting`s
So appealing.
It really
Has no ceiling.

My son though
Is very good.
At painting things
Made of wood.
Pastel painting
Was good fun.
Until he started
Eating one.

*Soon I'll be
Mister Fox.
Then my name
Will tick the box.
My son though
Might see red.
He'll be Basil
Brush instead....*

Who`s Driving Nora Batty

Keep in step
Compo please.
*I still fancy
Cheddar cheese.*
I enjoy
Wensleydale.
When your socks
Don't prevail.

*Nora washed
My dirty shirt.*
Were you trying
Hard to flirt.
*When I told her
I'm a swinger.
Said she'll put it
Through the wringer.*

*When taking her
Some boxes there.
I'd already
Washed my hair.
Then after showing
Me a tin.
We started putting
Curlers in.*

Wally backed
Another horse.
When Nora was
Out of doors.
Spoiling though
His winning run.
She came in
At ten to one.

*Nora comes
Out to bloom.
When she`s sweeping
With her broom.
Then a carpet
Does she beat.
Watching her
Is such a treat.*

*After playing
Once a Dame.
I was never
Quite the same.
When dying,
All my roots.
I became
The Puss in Boots.*

Compo, find
Yourself a bike!
Marina now
You're sounding like!
If buying Nora
One as well.
Would she let me
Ring her bell.

You see Foggy
I'm alright.
Nora still
Is my delight.
But Wally gets
All the luck.
When her stockings
Come unstuck.

Now I sell
A range of clothes.
Marina's paying
Through the nose.
After drinking
Summer wine.
I showed her my,
Bikini line....

The Rock Feature

Coming off
The beat for weeks.
Took some colour
From my cheeks.
Paint thieves
Were disbanded.
After catching
Them red handed.

Armed robbers
Would you know.
Once struck
Across Bow.
But info given
Wasn't hot.
So, became
A long shot.

Gang catching
Wasn't simple.
Though the leader
Had a dimple.
The getaway driver
Known as Prune.
Had been running
Loose since June.

Tired feet
Were feeling low.
With a certain
Pain in tow.
The cuffed leader
Wasn't speaking.
Nor a sentence
Was he seeking.

Court action
Started late.
When he called
The judge a mate.
Then after giving
Me some lip.
Started talking
With a zip.

Needing air
With my lawyer.
Can I talk
To Mr. Sawyer.
To run over
With a try.
If there is
An alley by.

*Judging how
You've fallen short!
A longer stretch
For you I've bought!
As stealing dough
You find fulfilling!
Less per roll
You will be given!*

Dealers we
Had to crack.
Were no jokers
In the pack.
From low living
Prison scrubs.
To the top
Ten of clubs.

Travelling out
A stiff we found.
With legs up
And head in ground.
The neck circled
With some boulders.
Carried the world
Upon his shoulders.

Acting roles
He could've done.
Like Rocky Two
Was there for one.
Or maybe later
Tried his hand.
Playing in
A rock band.

Thinking though
Very candid.
He was like
A missile landed.
Maybe later
With a plan.
Someone said
Rock it man.

Circling around
The village base.
Seemed like
A pizza place.
Inside we found
A dealer`s friend.
Had topped himself
In the end.

Bags laid
Near a wall.
But no drugs
Were there at all.
The other squad
In their stings.
Often make
A hash of things.

Nearby though
A woman laid.
With a pizza
Badly made.
Being assaulted
Was remote.
With pepper only
On her coat.

Even though
She seemed OK.
Soon went
On to say.
Although I`m nearly
Out of speed.
I'm better
Now I've weed.

Needing then
A casting vote.
To carry on
Or rock the boat.
The nose nearly
Passed it through.
But the eyes
Were level too.

After hearing
From HQ.
About another
Job to do.
A hamlet's where
We had to go.
To arrest
A Smoking Joe.

Down a hole
I nearly fell.
But didn't stop
Me wishing well.
Glue smelling
Dense and thick.
Led us to
A walking stick.

Drug smoke
Rose a lot.
Smelling like
Some chimney pot.
Though houses were
Alike and smart.
Washing lines
Were poles apart.

If ID's
To be cracked.
Is Rocket Man
There intact.
Would his head
Be in place.
Are there moles
Upon his face.

After then
A lengthy hush.
We came across
A chimney brush.
Smoking Joe
Was fast asleep.
Then we found
Sooty and Sweep.

A Tale of Two Kitties

Cats arriving
Night and day.
Think our lawn's
A litter tray.
And I'm living
Here in Fife.
Having kittens
With the wife.

Freddy`s really
Quite obtuse!
Fouling there
On the loose!
As our tortoise
Needing luck!
Once again.
Is getting stuck!

Fido's really
Quite a mate.
He patrols
The garden gate.
Which he learnt
From a pup.
But then started
Cocking it up.

Cats click
With Ginger well.
And his collar
Mating bell.
Often queuing
For a prize.
When demand
Is on the rise.

Ginger's never
Time to lose.
Straight away
He lights the fuse.
Last time
His bell rang!
There was one
Almighty bang!

Tails between
Certain legs.
Didn't include
The one who begs.
Then Fido watching
Ginger yawn.
Laid his keys
Upon the lawn.

Freddie's looking
Bold as brass!
Dropping more
Onto the grass!
As our tortoise
Nervous Noodle.
Gets counselled
By a Poodle.

Noodle has
A shiny roof.
Which he keeps
Weather proof.
Although he seems
A clever one.
He couldn`t make
A chicken run.

My hosepipe
Really flows!
Spraying up
In Freddie's nose!
And dodging more
Nasty crap.
Fido once
Caught the clap.

Noodle goes
Into his shell.
To escape
His living hell.
Then turning back
Into the hall.
Finds damp
Along the wall.

Ginger`s now
Dropping more.
Noodle's locked
His back door!
Then sees through
His periscope.
The poodle's off
To buy some soap.

Coming back
From the shop.
Were some kids
Drinking pop.
Hearing then
Wakey dad.
A cat nap
I must've had.

Let`s Enjoy A Happy Landing

So, Ern
Now It`s time.
For our show
Set in rhyme.
Don`t forget
I need support!
You are wearing
It I thought.

Your war play`s
A merry dance.
And could be
Your final chance.
Stretcher bearers
Though I`d say.
Started getting
Carried away.

Although it starts
At Biggin Hill.
Where small parts
Aren`t for Jill.
The landing strip
Was looking good.
From down stairs
Where I stood.

Cloud Cuckoo
Is your part.
It wasn't though
A flying start.
After eating
Milk Tray.
I didn't put
The chocs away.

Then yesterday
In the breeze.
I parachuted
In some trees.
Although I suffered
There I'd say.
The beech nuts
Faired ok.

Have you learnt
The story line.
Only when
I'm drinking wine.
Thinking about
Pilot Darking.
Dog fighting,
Over Barking.

*By the time
I woke today.
The Germans had
All gone away.
And last eggs
Went to Campbell.
So, I shouldn`t
Have to scramble.*

You`ll meet
Norman Dee.
A French spy
By the sea.
Words though
Will be few.
*Overheard
Could be the two.*

Near a pier
There you`ll find.
Careful though
He speaks his mind.
*That`s why
That lucid flutist.
Fell out with
A parachutist.*

The fish wife
Has a mole.
Oh yes
The Dover soul.
She wed Norman`s
Half-brother.
Pierre Duvet
Who`s undercover.

The Channel is
A dangerous place!
Yes Ern
I`ve seen your face.
Watching there
With Aunt Nelly.
Andy Pandy
On the telly.

Eric you`ll
Need disguise.
If you meet
Some German guys.
A new address
Then you`ll get.
Trousers are
A safer bet.

*I`m really
Sorry Ern.
I`ve better
Things to learn.*
What`s the problem
Do explain.
*The landing lights
Are on again….*

I`ll Let My Rhubarb Do The Talking

To understand
Fruit and veg.
I am here
To make a pledge.
Then you`ll see
How caulies bite.
And carrots in
A different light.

With my face
New to you.
I`m a Swede
Who`s feeling blue.
People often
Call me Ian.
And my wife
Is Olive Green.

Could some melons
Cause you doubt.
Can you work
Your sweetcorn out.
Do mushrooms cause
A darker thought.
Or are you
The fungi sort.

Are you wishing
Now somewhere.
Your last apple
Was a pear.
When singing
With a plumb.
Had Granny Smith
Been on the rum.

If scrumping
Apples make.
An addiction
Hard to break.
For plans
To really hatch.
I used
A cabbage patch.

Are you more
A fruit cake.
Does your wife
Like to bake.
After drinking
Up her sherry.
Is she more
A merry berry.

If you hear
A raspberry sound.
Twist and turn
Your feet around.
When your shoes
Are really done.
Banana slippers
Could be fun.

Keeping things
Fairly brief.
Would you wear
A fig leaf.
Should MP`s
Standing tall.
Now start
To lettuce all.

If you`re looking
For a stunner.
Now your bean
Has done a runner.
But charisma
Isn`t working.
Find yourself
A pickled gherkin.

I`ll return
Next week.
Showing people`s
Longest leek.
And ask why
Most of these.
Tend to go
For garden peas.

Your Crackers My Lord

Our new butler's
Full of cheek.
I'll replace him
By next week.
He`s a real
Sweetie Bert.
But starters dear!
Come as dessert!

Your bubbly
With no ice.
Thanks Claud
Your drinks are nice.
Show class!
I'm getting bored!
Oh yes
Your bitter my Lord.

My Lady It`s
A real delight.
Your desserts
Are just right.
Praising Claud
You've never done!
And you`ve my Lord
A sticky one.

He'll surely
Have to go!
Why did I
Recruit him though!
Don't forget
Your latest fancy!
Taking on
His sister Nancy!

Your deer
With no fat.
Gravy too,
I'm loving that!
Hurry Man!
I'm hungry Claud!
Oh yes
Your fowl my Lord.

He's rude!
That's for sure!
Calm down
I do implore!
Have you any
Ribs Claud!
Every bone
You've picked my Lord.

By the way
Tomorrow pet.
I nearly
Did forget.
Walking Brutus
You're no fan.
But you'll need
To carry the can.

Without being
Too specific.
My appointment's
At the clinic.
The chambermaid
Volunteered.
But she's new
And disappeared.

How will I
Pull the lead!
And which clinic,
Do you need!
Mussels here
Thank you, Claud.
And you have
Crabs my Lord….

I Must Catch Up on Some Sauce

Granville there's
Tea in pot.
Yes, but was
The kettle hot.
You on oath
Have my word.
Has it though
Been deferred.

Morning there
Missus Brown.
Although you seem
A little down.
You've today's
List in hand.
Instead of leaning
Where you stand.

Michael's in
Lots of pain!
And you`ve delivered
Wrong again!
He didn't want
Spotted Dick!
Take this cream
Away on tick.

Please Granville
Take some care!
Or she might
Go elsewhere!
Don`t though
Let her win.
Or she'll try
To rub it in.

Seeing Gladys
Though tonight.
Chances will
Be very slight.
When she says
Go where you like.
I'm riding your
Delivery bike.

Cooking though
Meat and rice.
Worries me
About the price.
So, I'll do
Something lentil.
Just to be
Experimental.

Hello again
Mister Stammers.
Sorry to hear
About the hammers.
Especially after
Recent matches.
And their pur
Purple patches.

Sorry Mister
Blenkinsop.
Dogs are banned
From the shop.
He works hard
Guiding me.
Couldn`t he
Though find a tree.

Granville she's
In my dreams.
But we play
For different teams.
And even though
I try to win.
I never get
My tackle in.

You dating
Buxom Trish.
Could result
In cheaper fish.
Although her skirt
Didn`t match.
Fish net stockings
Had no catch.

Although dwarfing
Me to her.
Many senses
I do stir.
Like our kettles
Never do.
Now she works
And whistles too.

A Flush with The Law

Mopping floors
And cleaning things.
Doesn`t come
With any strings.
But toilet cleaning`s
Quite a riddle.
When a person`s
On the fiddle.

Although my name
Is Dirty Dean.
This floor`s never
Mister Clean.
Though yesterday
I`m the man.
Who saw
A flash in the pan.

Horse racing
Is my love.
When placing bets
I win enough.
A jockey though
I`d love to be.
A stable lad
Is never me.

The vicar`s been
Once again.
And pointed at
The porcelain.
Others standing
Laughed away.
When he said
Let us spray.

Arthur`s boring
Me again.
His aching leg
Becomes a drain.
A lonely man
Of sixty-three.
Who`s postcode
Is WC.

Someone of
A lewd type.
Looking for
Some pickings ripe.
Led to bribing me
Me for ten.
When I said
Come later then.

Friendly copper
Simon Drake.
Often likes
To have a shake.
Last time
He closed a case.
The broken zip
He couldn`t trace.

I explained
A crafty man.
Acting like
A Desperate Dan.
Will return
Here to flout.
So, you could
Flush him out.

When his boss
Half awake.
Find he`s bribed
A certain fake.
There inside
He`ll be caught.
Ending with
A fallen short.

Retuning for
The lesser said.
He`s blushing like
My tenner red.
Which I`ll take
To invest.
Arthur`s back
For another rest.

Three Kind Mice, See How They Pun

So then
We`ve made it Jill
Climbing up
This blooming hill.
Although I like
The summer breeze.
Shame about
When you sneeze.

The grass looks
Inviting here.
If Jack
You`d volunteer.
Polly`s though
Tea and cream.
Is the way
To let off steam.

How come
You`re asking me.
Bobby Shafto`s
Gone to sea.
Well keep away
From that ram.
As Mary had
A little lamb.

Loving Humpty
I abide.
Especially with
His sunny side.
Slipping though
On some oil.
Got himself
A nasty boil.

*Don`t forget
Doctor Foster.
Goes hunting
Here in Gloucester.
After being
Sacked he begs.
And yesterday
Was poaching eggs.*

*Thinking he`d
Become a vet.
Fizzy drink
Made him forget.
Then after sadly
Drinking diesel.
He tried to pop
My brother`s weasel.*

Jack Spratt
Is coming clean.
His wife eats
On the lean.
Then farmer
Hay Diddle,
Said their cat
Is on the fiddle.

Farmer Diddle
Wasn`t meek.
When he did
That funny streak.
I remember
Last June.
The cow jumped
Over the moon.

*Old King
Cole, you know.
Seems a funny
So and so.
When sitting
On the throne.
He never liked
To be alone.*

*Now he lodges
In a shoe.
With a woman
That is true.
Although he fixed
The garden gate.
Her tongue though
Is never straight.*

*Then he said
Holy Moses.
I`ve found
A ring of Roses.*
Is it on
Her finger now.
*No, he swapped it
For a cow.*

The pie man`s
A happy soul.
When he`s made
A sausage roll.
Often humour
Does he revel.
Now his table
Isn`t level.

He saw
Marjorie Daw.
Steal a clock
From number four.
Then chasing her
Around the block.
Led her to
The Hickory Dock.

Knowing his
Latest rhyme.
Won`t support
Her doing time.
Although he`d like
To save her bacon.
To Upson Downs
She`ll be taken.

The water well
Is her Jack.
So, we better
Take some back.
Wait Jill
Just a minute!
The pale I
Forgot to bring it!

Fifty Shades of Ray

Stealing cars
You`ve never done!
Tonight though
We`re needing one!
For Little John
It must be good!
Will I need
A robbing hood?

Before driving
Far away!
Check your exit
Is OK!
Certain places
Are a bind.
Crinkly Bottom
Comes to mind.

Which kind
Would you swipe?
I`m looking for
A sporty type.
If she doesn`t
Want to play.
Could I have
Her number Ray.

You`re becoming
Such a drag!
Last week
I stole a Jag.
The engine started
Pinking mind.
That`s OK
I`m colour blind.

Passing on
To London boys!
They demand
All the toys!
Blue tooth
Pleases well.
What about
A root canal.

An Aston Martin
That`ll do.
We could steal it
Me and you.
Maybe M
Would be stirred.
Unless she had
The final word.

You`re grinding
All my gears!
And increasing
Many fears!
Nothing`s working
Here though Ray.
Can`t it Die
Another Day.

Lucky shades
Here I sport.
Save me
From getting caught.
Are we talking
Very long.
From this morning
Going strong.

This morning
What`s your game!
That`s no time
From dodging blame!
Luck though
I surely bought.
When stealing them
I wasn't caught.

Electric cars
Aren`t for me.
Someone though
Has left the key.
If we`re later
Still at large.
Will they place
An extra charge.

Now I`ve lost
The blooming key!
So, losing time
We shall be!
If it was
Inside your ear.
A head start
Would see us clear.

A copper`s walking
Up this way.
He`s the one
I saw today.
To the station
I was taken.
Where I managed
To save my bacon.

Chatting him
A friendly line.
With your shades
We`ll be fine.
No, he needs
To pass quick!
His sun glasses
I did nick!

The Out of Time Team

On day three
Here we`re sat.
Having a laugh
About Phil`s hat.
A seagull took it
With no grace.
Causing Phil
To flap and chase.

Feeling now
So undressed.
His morale
Is not the best.
To resume
On Sussex land.
Where the downs
Were not planned.

Last week
Near a cavern.
Phil came
Across a tavern.
Then sounding like
Angela Merkel.
Walked in
A stoned circle.

Although a rash
On his chest.
Left him feeling
Not the best.
A skeleton find
Long departed.
Left him itching
To get started.

Was he Phil
The fighting kind.
*It's very hard
To read his mind.*
Being noble
Would he pass?
*He must've joined
A slimming class.*

*He wouldn't be
Full of beans.
After seeing
Battle scenes.
But may've told
Certain fibs.
About disliking
Spare ribs.*

Was he strong
And very brave.
*He must`ve had
A close shave.*
Was it key
To being crocked.
*Hard to say
His jaw is locked.*

Though geophys
Made it clear.
The Roman villa
Wasn`t near.
Phil`s looking
Up at last.
After digging
Up the past.

Digger driver
Steven Lee.
Is standing now
Behind a tree.
Singing there
Like a pro.
Helping all
The acorns grow.

Sadly we`ve
Lost the race.
And Phil`s tripped
Over his lace.
You`ve a talent
That I know.
My comfy hat
I`m missing though.

Steven then
From the heart.
Said to Phil
Where do I start?
Because she left
Her clothes behind.
My seagull will
Be hard to find….

Saturday Plight Fever

Dancing here
Is right for me.
But people seem
To disagree.
And even though
I`m turbo driven.
When I twist
I`m unforgiven.

Moon Walking
Gave me cramp.
With feet talking
Like a champ.
Then a lady
Like before.
Took the Michael
On the floor.

Having though
Charm to burn.
I deserve
A fare return.
Although I failed
A dance class.
Any bus
I`m free to pass.

Even when
I had a stroke.
My spirit never
Really broke.
But when dancing
In the mix.
Maybe then
I need a fix.

When my wig
Mad a splash.
Me and puddles
Had a clash.
But my failing
With the girls.
Needs a chest
With longer curls.

The crowded floor
Was fever pitch.
But my nose
Had an itch.
Scratching though
I really think.
YMCA
Was out of sync.

A missing lens
I was searching.
On all fours
Had me lurching.
A pair of draws
Was the best.
Reminder though
About my chest.

Meeting then
A lovely bird.
With my senses
Nicely stirred.
I said,
Once or twice.
A brief encounter
Would be nice.

But her reply
I didn`t like.
When she said
On your bike.
Then after strutting
With some pace.
Called me then
A spanner case.

Then, home I took
An English Rose.
When eating bread
She did repose.
I like dancing
With some clout.
But bloomers I
Can do without.

Bubble bath
I do enjoy.
So why not
You older boy.
And even though
Your name is Terry.
You sparkle
Like a perry.

Something though
I had to say.
Made the bubbles
Go away.
When I told her
You`ll discover.
Billie Jean
Was not your mother....

Was It Wise To Go To Morecambe

Sorry Ern
You`re a late.
Arriving here
At heaven`s gate.
Angels though
Are doing fine.
On my cloud
Number nine.

Room here
Is getting short.
According to
An astronaut.
Was he then
Kind of famous.
No, he spoke
About Uranus.

So, where Ernie
Did it end?
In a field
With a friend.
A bullock saw me
Chewing grass.
Then I wondered
Would it pass.

But it came
After me.
As I ran
Towards a tree.
Ending in
A mighty smash.
So, this urn
Is full of ash.

*Home visits
Happen Ern.
If you do
A star turn.
The farmer though
Isn`t now.
Into Stella
At the Plough.*

*Drinking here`s
A decent bet.
As caught short
I never get.
And to think
When I passed.
Cloudy cider
Was my last.*

*After finding
Benny Hill.
Fast asleep
And very still.
Buxom angels
On the make.
Allowed him
To hold a wake.*

*Delivering milk
Seemed a guise.
When he ran it
Passed your eyes.*
How did Benny
Meet his end.
*Trapezing badly
With a friend.*

Have you any
Menthol sweets.
*No but angels
Give out treats.
But before
I came to heaven.
Gave tunes
To Andre Previn.*

Where am I
Supposed to eat.
*Cloud one
Is hard to beat.
Caviar`s
The way to go.
Never twice
Though in a row.*

*And down below
I can see.
Fish fingers
At number three.*
Are your glasses
Seeing true.
*Yes, I get
A Birds Eye view.*

Going by
What you said.
Will I be
Cavia fed.
*No, I told
A certain lie.
Pie though
Was in the sky….*

Has My Talent Gone To Waste

Bins to empty
By the score.
Feels like
The grand tour.
And number tens
Holy Moses.
Never leaves
A smell of roses.

Driver Kate`s
A pretty sort.
Who`s really
Quite a sport.
And her figure`s
Looking great.
So now enjoys
A blind date.

Being a model
Was her dream.
But could never
Quite redeem.
The catwalk
Made her glum.
Down the lane
She stood in some.

The other one
Swinger Gwyn.
Likes dancing
With a bin.
When he tells
A joke or two.
And this week
Are very blue.

Crafty Dave
Is wearing thin.
Leaving glue
Upon his bin.
When venting
Our displeasure.
Every time
We stick together.

Carol`s quite
A car fan.
Who`s looking
For a man.
And it`s very
Nice to stop.
When she`s in
Her open top.

Once appearing
In The Sun.
Took her straight
To number one.
Then yesterday
I told her that.
Her tyres though
Were looking flat.

All sorts
Do we meet.
And Bertie Basset`s
Very sweet.
Though last week
Psycho Sid.
Once again
Flipped his lid.

Stopping for
A bite to eat.
Gwyn`s smile
Is hard to beat.
He seems
A happy chap.
After reading
On his app.

Join me
For a date.
My name
Is Cosy Kate.
Call me soon
With some haste.
I`ve a new
Recycled waist.

Printed in Great Britain
by Amazon